Technical Writing

The Complete Beginners' Guide.

Solomon Eseme

Technical Writing: The Complete Guide

With an average of **$78,060** annually according to the U.S. BUREAU OF LABOR STATISTICS, technical writing is a term you need to look into.

The term is attributed to those who create content explaining a particular technology and /or its usage.

If you love writing and technology, you're on the right track to becoming a technical writer.

We will explore technical writing in-depth and get you started creating your first technical content.

Enjoy!

Sincerest,

Solomon Eseme

Table of Contents

What is Technical Writing?   4

Benefits of Technical Writing   6

Who is a Technical Writer?   7

Types of Technical Writers   7

What does a technical writer do?   8

Technical Writer Skill Set?   9

How to Become a Good Technical Writer?   10

Types of Technical Writing   11

The Technical Writing Process   14

Technical Writing Niches   25

Top Technical Writing Tips   30

Technical Writing Resources   32

Technical Writing Jobs   33

About Solomon

Solomon Eseme is a Full Stack Engineer, Technical Writer, Developer Advocate, and the Founder of Masteringbackend, Sayonne, and Unihux

Solomon Eseme is a developer with over 7 years of active and professional software engineering experience. Developing innovative applications with programming languages such as JavaScript, PHP, and Java.

He started coding as a Technical Educator. He has experience explaining complex technical concepts through Teaching, Writing, and Speaking.

Solomon Eseme has worked as a freelance technical writer with exciting tech startups and companies such as LogRocket, Strapi, Kinsta, Vonage, and LambdaTest, etc to create technical content, documentation, Knowledge-based content, etc.

Solomon Eseme has also spoken at different events organized by different communities such as GDG, ForLoop Africa, DevFest, Backend Community, Twitter Spaces, and other online events.

Prologue

My technical writing journey started with twists, turns, and even a short slippery slide down the path of depression.

It had a lot to do with criticism — the very fuel that kills the greatest ideas in the world and stops them from ever materializing.

But guess what? I didn't let the harsh criticism stop me from publishing my first paper and to this day, that paper remains the cornerstone of my success as a technical writer.

While you may face some difficulty embarking on your journey as a technical writer, especially if this is "alien terrain" for you, you're sure to win if you keep this in mind:

"You can do anything"

That said, take the time to read this short book. You'll learn the principles of technical writing and all you need to do to become one.

For good measure, I'll repeat: "You can do anything"

See you at the next one.

Solomon Eseme

What is Technical Writing?

Technical writing is a form of writing that translates complex technical topics into easily digestible and understandable content.

It covers a pattern of writing where the writer writes on a particular subject that requires breaking down the complex part of the subject to its simplest form by giving direction, instruction, or explanation about that subject matter.

Technical writing comes with a different style, it carries a different purpose and involves different characteristics that are different from other writing styles such as creative writing, business writing, or academic writing.

Some examples of technical writing are discussed in this book under Technical writing Niches.

Benefits of Technical Writing

The benefit of technical writing is enormous and cannot be over-emphasized, also technical writing benefits both companies and technical writers in different ways and we are going to explore each of them.

Companies

The benefits of technical writing to companies are massive if done right. Listed below are the common benefits companies can derive from technical writing.

Educate your end-users

In this digital and information age, educating your end-users should be the utmost priority of companies as it builds trust among users.

According to the book "*The Thank You Economy by Marcus Sheridan*", When you educate your users, your users trust you and they buy from you and also refer their friends.

Therefore, investing in your user's education through technical writing is a win-win game for your company

Keep customers informed and satisfied

If your support is filled with repeated questions concerning a particular task in your product, maybe it's time to create technical contents around those questions and see how your support volume will reduce drastically.

With enough technical content that answers different technical questions of your customers, the more they are well informed and satisfied.

To individuals

As a technical writer, you can benefit in several ways too, and below is a list of common ways you can benefit as a technical writer.

1. Technical writing improves your communication skills. Technical writing right away demonstrates how inflated one's image of communication skills is. This leads to self-improvement if we decide to improve our communication game.
2. Technical writing is a writing niche with high demand and high pay as well, especially if you know how to do any structural authoring or API documentation.
3. Technical writing teaches you to be a keen observer of events and actions and pay attention to details. Attention to detail is an important soft skill and technical writing helps you to improve it.
4. Technical writing helps you organize your thoughts clearly and also improves your articulation. You quickly get into the habit of making lists and constructing tree-view diagrams while writing. This skill to organize information improves all other parts of one's life and helps us live more productive lives.
5. Technical writing helps you to understand technology better and thus increases your capacity to adapt to new waves of technologies. That's the technically empowering aspect of technical writing.
6. As a software engineer and a technical writer, you can easily transition to different career paths such as Developer Advocacy, Staff Technical Writer, Technical Content Manager, etc.

The benefits of technical writing to companies and individuals are enormous and create with a sense of fulfillment for both parties. Next, let's explore who the technical writer is and what they do in their day-to-day life.

Who is a Technical Writer?

A Technical writer is a skilled wordsmith that converts complex technical information into easily readable technical content. This technical content can be in the form of documentation, whitepapers, howtos, user guides, manuals, blog posts, etc.

There are different types of technical writers based on the type of content that they produce. In the next section, we are going to explain the two major types.

Type of Technical Writers

There are different types of technical writers based on the following criteria: job title, type of content, etc.

Fig. 1.0 – Type of technical writers

We will group them into two broad types viz:

1. Staff Technical Writer
2. Freelance Technical Writer

Staff Technical Writer

This title houses all the technical writers working in a company as staff. No matter the different job titles or seniority positions. This set of technical writers focuses more on creating technical content for the specific company they are working with.

The type of content they create includes documentation, howtos, user guides and manuals, instructions, technical blog posts, Product Requirement Documents(PRD), etc.

Freelance Technical Writer

Freelance technical writers focus more on creating technical content for clients as either a contract base or one-time payment.

They can also create different types of content such as documentation, whitepapers, manuals, step-by-step how-to guides, and technical blog post; but the difference is that they manage their business and processes.

However, you need to understand what technical writers do in their day-to-day careers.

Technical Writing: The Complete Guide

What does a technical writer do?

A technical writer is responsible for creating content. This technical content can range from journal articles, technical and instructional manuals, and training guides, to assessments.

Imagine the different titles a technical writer can have such as tech writer, technical communicator, etc. They all produce technical content or manage other technical writers.

Additionally, the type of technical content produced may differ based on the targeted niche or based on the company's requirements.

However, as part of enhancing the end-users experience with the products, technical writers sometimes work with product liability specialists, customer service managers, and user experience experts to enhance the quality of their content.

Next, we will explore the skills you should have to become a technical writer. This will give you insight into how to become a technical writer.

Technical Writing: The Complete Guide

Technical Writer Skill Set?

Technical writing cuts through different fields of study such as Technical Communication, Engineering, and Computer Science. Therefore, there are many skills you should have to become a technical writer and it is summarized into 2 broad categories.

Writing Skills

The most important skill of a technical writer is learning how to communicate effectively through writing.

The main duty of a technical writer is to explain complex technical terms in readable content or documentation which is the most important factor that determines you as a good technical writer.

Therefore, a technical writer needs to learn how to convey meaning through writing, and how to structure technical content with proper punctuation, tenses, voices, etc that conveys meaning to the target audience.

Technological Skills

Becoming a technical writer requires a certain skill and domain knowledge in technology.

Technical Writing: The Complete Guide

You can either know any of these fields or any field not listed below that is related to technology in general

1. Software engineering
2. Product Manager
3. Project manager
4. QA engineers
5. Data and business analysts
6. Product designers

If you have domain knowledge in the above technological path listed above, it may accelerate your learning process in becoming a technical writer.

Nevertheless, becoming a technical writer does not ultimately depend on your knowledge of technology as everything is learnable

As stated above, the main duty of a technical writer is to explain complex technical terms in readable content or documentation which is the most important factor that determines you as a good technical writer.

Therefore, learning or knowing how to write and structure your content to explain complex technical terms in the simplest form possible becomes the most sought-after skill of a technical writer.

So, anyone without the above domain knowledge can become a technical writer provided they know how to write and are willing to learn along the journey.

How to Become a Good Technical Writer?

No matter the aspect of technical writing you focus on, now that you have the required skills that guarantee you to become a technical writer, how do you become a good technical writer, or what makes a good technical writer?

Fig. 1.3 – How to become a good technical writer?

As we stated earlier, you aim to simplify complex subject matter; so applying these steps helps you provide clear instructions and directions that are self-explanatory for any reader going through your writing.

Technical Writing: The Complete Guide

Know your audience.

Getting to know the audience that would be consuming your writing helps you narrow the terms, abbreviations, acronyms, etc. used in your writing to correspond to that used in such a field of study.

And if the people going to be reading your writing are beginners or novices, knowing this helps you put your writing in a manner where every detail is explained and spelled out for them to be able to understand and apply.

Use a third-person perspective.

Second person is basic to modern professional technical writing. Third person has an occasional role too.

In some cases, you want to make sure your writing uses a third-person perspective so you don't unprofessionally address the reader.

See yourself as a teacher instructing a student, therefore get rid of any personal opinion unless necessary. When writing, you must make your point by providing your reader with enough detail with fewer and clear words.

Research

Researching is one of the major skills you need to develop as a technical writer. Your ability to seek information from several sources, study and understand the information gathered, and then move on to analyze the information thoroughly, and then write down the information in a simple pattern that the readers would be able to understand.

Types of Technical Writing

Technical writing is a very detail-oriented writing field where advanced knowledge is required.

Fig. 1.2 – Types of technical writing

It is categorized into these 3 broad categories or its assignments normally take one of these forms.

- End-user documentation
- Traditional technical writing
- Technical marketing communications

End-user Documentation

The End-user documentation also known as **customer-oriented documentation** provides instructions for the end user of a given product. The instructions are laid in such a way that it is easier to understand by non-technical users.

Here are some of the key technical writing examples of end-user documentation:

- User manuals or user guides
- FAQ sections
- Documentations
- Knowledge bases
- Company wikis
- Online help centers
- How-to guides
- Setup and installation guide

Traditional technical writing

Traditional technical writing is a concept where content is written by an audience with specific expertise for their peers.

It is also called **Expert to expert tech documentation or freelance technical writing**.

This concept is used largely in technical writing where freelance technical writers with a certain expert level in technologies or proven knowledge of technical writing are contracted to write detailed content for companies.

This is where freelance technical writers become very relevant. Companies are increasingly in demand of expert technological-related content to create content for them based on their experience using a specific technology or technical content related to how these technical writers use their products.

You can learn how to create your freelance technical writers portfolio to attract high-paying clients.

Here are a few examples of traditional technical writing:

- Technical blog posts
- Online Articles
- Knowledge base
- Tutorials
- How-to Guides
- Technical specs and API documentation

Technical marketing communications

These are technical writers who contribute to the marketing materials of a product or company at large. These technical writers need to communicate their expertise in a more user-friendly language to help the prospective buyer understand and take an interest in the product.

This is related to the term "Product-led technical writing", which has to do with writing and structuring your technical content to attract leads, buyers, and customers to a specific product.

This area of technical writing houses many names such as technical content marketing, technical marketing, technical content manager, etc.

Here are a few examples of technical marketing communications:

- White papers
- Surveys
- Marketing-related case studies
- Business plans
- Product Reviews

This type of content promotes a product or service to the desired audience. The technical writing process differentiates the different types of technical writing listed above. Let's explore the technical writing process in the next section.

The Technical Writing Process

Defining a technical writing process is subjective and it depends on the type of content and the technical writer. It is a process you follow to produce high-quality technical content. We will look at and also modify the lean process created by Linda Ikechukwu from *Everything Technical Writing*.

Fig. 1.3 – The technical writing process

This process is very simple and covers everything you need to produce steady, high-quality technical content.

Define your audience

When you have a technical content idea or proposed topic to work on. The first thing you need is to research the audience that intends to consume your technical content.

This knowledge lays a clear path for you to determine the tone, voice, and sense of the technical content.

It is more impressive to write for a specific target audience than to try to cover everyone. This makes your technical content more impactful and useful to that unique audience.

Here are some of the questions you need to ask yourself when determining the specific audience you're targeting.

1. Who am I writing this piece of content for?
2. Are they beginners, advanced, experts, etc?
3. What is their profession(Developers, designers, etc)
4. What knowledge is required before reading this technical content?

There are more questions, but these will help guide you toward developing a reader's personal opinion of your technical content.

Define the goal of the content

The next important factor is to determine the goal of your technical content before you even start writing. This helps you stay on track instead of straying away from the main goal of the technical content.

The most important factor of every technical content you produce is to provide value. The value you want to provide in the technical content will determine how you structure the content.

For instance, if you want to create technical content that shows a reader how to build a product with Y technology.

From the goal, you will understand that you will show code samples, show step by step guide with the knowledge obtained from determining the goal of your technical content, and your content will be structured or presented in a way that delivers value appropriately.

To determine the goal of your technical content, you can ask yourself these questions:

1. What will the reader achieve from reading the content?
2. What value will my readers gain from this technical content?
3. What problem will my readers be able to solve after reading this technical content?

Above all, you need to determine what your readers expect or what they will benefit from reading your technical content.

Define your content brief

Content briefs are very important to give you context for the type of technical content you are creating.

A content brief is a summary of what the content is supposed to achieve, the audience definition, the primary and secondary keywords, the goal of the technical content, competitors' content to draw insights, etc.

This document is the result of the above research for defining your audience and defining the goal of the technical content.

However, companies pre-writers this document to give the writers context as to what the company wants the technical content to cover.

Nevertheless, writers create content briefs to help them stay focused on to show the company what they intend to cover in the article.

Here is an example of the Content Brief format I use for all my clients.

Fig. 1.4 – A sample of custom brief

Write an outline

A content outline gives a clear direction of what the final content will look like. It is like a map that guides you to a destination.

As a technical writer, you must invest a little time in developing a great content outline for your technical content.

I use this approach to produce high-quality technical content faster.

To produce a great template for your content outline, you need to follow this approach.

Every content outline should contain the following:

1. Content Outline Points
2. Content Outline sub-points

Content Outline Points

From the title of your technical content and the information you have gathered from the research and content brief, you should be able to split the content into main sections.

For instance, if you're writing the title: "Building Node App with Express.js"

From your research, you will understand that the content is for complete beginners and you need to lay a foundation of knowledge before proceeding to the actual coding of the Todo app.

So, you might want to define them in this format:

Title: Building Todo App with Express.js

Content Outline:

1. Introduction
2. Prerequisite
3. What is Express.js
4. Overview of the Todo app
5. Building a Todo App
6. Conclusion

Fig 1.5 Content Outline Main Point Sample (Source: content.ai)

This lays out the main points you intend to cover in your technical content. Next, to give more context to the main points, you can create a subheading to further simplify the points you intend to cover in the main heading.

Correct Outline sub-points

This contains different sub-points you intend to cover from each main point listed above. Let's take a look at the sample we are using.

Fig 1.6 Technical Content Outline Subpoint Sample(Source ....)

The example above gives you a clear picture of what the final content will contain. Structuring your content outline this way also helps you easily get back to the content idea if you left it for a while.

Do your research

This is where the work starts, now you have a clear understanding of the technical content you want to produce. The next step is to jump into extensive research about the technologies involved and how you intend to pass the value.

Research is a very important factor in producing high-quality content. That's why every good piece of content is split into 60% research, 10% writing, 10% editing, and 20% distribution.

Fig. 1.2 Content of a high-quality technical article

Technical Writing: The Complete Guide

Research is also a continuous process and it starts right from when you define the audience and the goal of the content, and come up with your content briefly when you're writing and editing.

Here is how you can start researching, if your content brief contains links to your competitor's content on the same topic, start from there.

Additionally, you can research through the top-ranking technical content on the same topic from any search engine of your choice.

After researching, studying, and understanding the technologies and gaining authority over the topic.

Next, you write down the following points:

- What is missing in the articles you researched?
- What interests you the most?
- Check the comment section for what readers are saying.
- How do they structure the content?
- What can you improve in the article?
- If coding is required, do it now to gain more insight.
- Group your research results accordingly.
- etc

With this, you have enough authority and are also ready to come up with your first draft of the content.

Write the first draft

Writing your first draft should not be that hard because, from your research, you already have enough knowledge, authority, and idea of what to write.

Also, your first draft is more of a brain dump. It's where you simply put down your ideas into writing without much consideration of grammar, structuring, etc.

Write down all the ideas related to the outline you have created for your content. If you get stuck at this stage, it's normal, you can pause and do more research and come back to it.

The goal here should be to get your ideas into writing as quickly as possible without considering grammar, structuring, etc.

Rewrite the first draft

Rewriting your first draft is aimed to organize your technical content in an acceptable or presentable format.

Here, you check the structure of the technical content and make sure it passes the value intended in the content brief, and at the same time, the tones, voices, and tenses align with the audience you define for your technical content.

It is recommended to include additional resources for your readers after reading your technical content. This is where you should take it further by including additional resources for your readers from the research you conducted.

These are some of the things you need to check when rewriting your first draft.

- Most importantly, you need to make sure your content is readable by rewriting each paragraph to align with your audience if necessary.
- Remove fluffs or paragraphs that deviate from your main point and stick to giving value to each paragraph.
- Make sure to drive the reader through each section with your closing remark on each section.

There are many things to do at this stage, but most importantly, your technical content should pass the desired value to the intended audience at this stage before you move to fine-tuning your content.

Fine-tune and polish

At this stage, you need to fine-tune your technical content to give da vet value without too many paragraphs, ambitious sentences, grammar, etc.

Here are some of the generic checklists of things you can do to improve your technical content.

Technical Writing: The Complete Guide

- Run content through Grammarly for incorrect spelling and grammar
- Create smooth transitions between paragraphs, sentences, and sections.
- Run plagiarism check on your technical content using Grammarly or Unicheck
- Break bigger paragraphs into a max of 4 lines.
- Remove awkward phrases or ambiguous words to promote understanding and readability.
- Make your headers brief and promote value.
- Break out sentences with more than 3 connections.
- Check all links for broken links.
- Check your conclusion to make sure it summarizes the content value

There is every chance that after all these, your technical content is still not in good shape. At this point, you need to ask for feedback from your peers or editor.

If you're a freelance technical writer, you can submit your first draft now and wait for feedback if you can't get an editor or any peer.

Ask for feedback

Asking for feedback is a great way to learn and grow in the field of writing and the same applies to technical writing.

To become a great writer, you need a great editor that gives you constructive criticism and also helps you align your content to the right tone, voice, style goals, etc.

If you have a friend or an editor, this is the stage to get in touch with them for a second or third-eye view of your technical content.

Discuss the feedback they provide to learn and inspire them to improve the technical content before publishing.

The folks at Technowriter are open to giving you constructive feedback on your technical content anytime. You can join our community to grow your technical writing career.

Publish and share

Content publishing and distribution is a broad topic to it covers 24% of your content journey.

If you're a freelance technical writer, write technical content for a company. The company will handle the publishing and maybe give you the link to your published content for your social platform promotion.

Also, if you write for yourself, this is the time to publish your content and share it with the world.

Whichever, Technowriter gives you a publishing tool that helps you auto-cross post your technical content on platforms such as Medium, Hashnode, Dev.to, WordPress, Strapi, and other CMS at once.

The tool also allows you to auto-share your content on your connected social media accounts.

Technical Writing Niches

Technical writing is aimed at audiences' understanding of how to use products. Every technical content targets a specific group/niche of people.

Below are different areas or types of technical content you can specialize in as a technical writer and produce.

User Guides

This is an instructional manual that directs the user on how to use and interact with a product. It details a step-by-step approach to how to use a particular product. This document is usually added to newly purchased items.

For online software, it is safe to say that the "Get Started" section of the documentation is the User Guide.

API Documentation

It is a document or a webpage that demonstrates how to interact, integrate or use the public API of a particular software product.

It shows tutorials, code snippets, references, classes, methods, format rules, and amongst others smart rules on how to use the public API. This document is a developer's guide to interacting with an API. API Documentation helps to

- Improves API versioning
- Increases API usage
- Provides a great user experience

Here is an ultimate guide to creating your own API author this Guide.

SDK Documentation (Software Development Kit)

Companies develop Software Development Kits to aid developers to get started with building and interacting with their APIs easily. This type of documentation includes creating instructional content on how to use the SDK.

It contains FAQs, library instructions, code snippets, and guides to using and working with the SDK.

Project Plans

These are documents used by project managers in project control and execution. It documents the stages involved in project management such as initiation, planning, execution, control, and conclusion.

This document helps project managers and stakeholders to:

- Track progress
- Improves project
- Provides structure and foresight

White Paper

A white paper is a written report to inform the uses of a problem and a valid solution to the problem.

In a white paper, there are convincing facts and evidence of the problem and the solution. It is used by companies, technical fields, governments, and businesses to provide a clear solution to a problem.

A White-paper helps to;

- Improve sales
- Increase engagement
- Establish expertise

Onboarding guides

This is a document that lists the required steps a new user needs to get familiar with a product.

It explains and shows how a product works, the necessary steps users should know, and the steps to take.

In most cases, the onboarding content trains the user, imparts their experiences, gives them insights into how to make the most use of the product, and guides them between basic and complex parts of the products.

How To guides and Technical Blogpost

This is informative technical content that is aimed at teaching users a particular subject or process. It shows a step-by-step guide to achieving a particular thing.

Freelance technical writers create technical blog posts or how-to guides to demonstrate how to use a particular technology or tool.

They are step-by-step tasks and expository pieces. An example of How to guide is a repair manual. It gives quick fixes and "Do-it-yourself" tasks.

Here is a guide to learning how to create how-to guides and technical blog post.

RFPS & Proposals

This document describes the entirety of the project and reports alternative solutions.

It discloses an intended project and requests funding. RFP focuses on investors, benefactors, and interested third parties.

Case Studies

They are expository writings and an in-depth study of a subject. They generalize over every unit of a subject matter. A brief piece to introduce products, and analyze a phenomenon, a person, or team of persons.

Standard Operating Procedures

Standard Operating Procedures (SOPs) are internal documents that aid employees in an organization to carry out their duties. It is rather and conveys ease of work and success.

They contain descriptive policies, procedures, and standards for the organization.

Test Schedules

This document is required in Agile methodologies, it includes test strategy, data requirements, and status of previous results.

It's a detailed document consisting of the objectives, descriptions, and procedure of a product.

Product Requirement Documentation

This is one of the most important documents in software engineering. It outlines the requirement of a product. It shows the details of each feature and how it relates to other features in the product.

It describes the product, tools, features, and deliverables. It's the product communication guide, outlining every detail and process of a product.

Market Requirements Documentation

A document that reports the details of the market(users). It describes the needs of users, target audiences, competitors, and market cap. It takes precedence over product requirements. It aids business analysis. MRD helps to:

- Understand trends and needs of users
- Reduce the risk of wasting resources
- Meet the needs of users
- Identify market opportunities

Release Note

This document encompasses every fix, upgrade, and process made to a product. It includes reports, product limitations, and upgraded features. Also, versions of the software are used for the product.

The release note also gives details of upgrades made to the product documentation.

A release note is released after product development. In some cases, it's released during development and it's called the "Beta Release".

Top Technical Writing Tips

Below are the top technical writing tips to help you become a good technical writer.

Fig. 1.8 – Technical writing tips

Just Start Writing

According to Jean M. Auel — "You learn to write by writing, and by reading and thinking about how writers have created their characters and invented their stories. If you are not a reader, don't even think about being a writer."

If you want to learn how to write, the best way is to start writing now. Pick up a challenge you recently solved and write about it.

You can create a free Medium, or Hashnode account to create your blog and start pushing out technical content.

Understand your audience

Before you publish an article, make sure you define who the technical content is for, and its goal.

This will help you structure your content properly as stated earlier in this article.

Embrace supporting imagery

"A picture is worth a thousand words" — Napoleon Bonaparte

As you write your content, you need to understand that your readers are busy and have a shorter attention span than ever before, and so you want to engage them by using a variety of assets.

You can try images, vectors, infographics, illustrations, etc to pass information more quickly than words.

Simplify your language

Analyze competitors' content

Don't use ambiguous and difficult-to-understand and grammar. Technical writing aims to break down complex technical terms into simple understandable content. You should try to stick with simple but correct English/ or any language!

Stay Consistent

You get better by writing more. The more technical content you put out there, the better you become at creating more content

You can set a content calendar for yourself and collaborate with a friend to stay accountable.

Join Writing Challenges

To stay consistent, be accountable, and improve your writing skills, you need to join many writing communities and participate in writing challenges such as the Hashnode Hack Writing Challenge, Contribute to Open Source projects, or join Google Season of Docs.

Technical Writing Resources

As a technologist, you can quickly get started with technical writing without any course or book, provided you know how to write and communicate your thoughts.

However, to stand out as an expert in the field, taking a course on technical writing is highly paramount because you will discover many tips that will help you become a better writer and technical writer.

Below is a list of recommended books you can take to become a better technical writer.

Books Resources

Below is a list of the top 5 technical writing books and recommended free resources you can take to become a better technical writer.

Free Books Resources

The free resources are available online for any technical writer to access and grow their technical writing careers.

Technical Writing: The Complete Guide

Google Technical Writing Course

This technical writing course from Google is highly recommended for complete beginners. It gives readers the foundation needed to excel in the field of technical writing.

Documenting APIs

This is a free guide to technical documentation by the idratherbewriting blog. It is the best free resource to learn API Documentation and I recommend checking it out.

Check the Documenting APIs: A guide for technical writers and engineers on the idratherbewriting blog.

Here is a list of selected free technical writing resources to hone your technical writing skills.

Let's explore the top 5 paid technical writing books that I will personally recommend you start reading now to grow your technical writing career.

Technical Writing: The Complete Guide

Paid Books Resources

Here are the top 3 most recommended paid books to grow your technical writing career.

Technical Writing Process

The Technical Writing Process is a simple 3-step guide that anyone can use to create technical documents such as user guides, manuals, and procedures. The book was written by Kieran Morgan, and co.

The Insider's Guide to Technical Writing

This is a must-read book for every technical writer as it helps explain complex technical concepts to users in an understandable format.

Every complex product needs to be explained to its users, and technical writers, also known as technical communicators, are the ones who do the job. In a growing field, technical writing requires multiple skills, including an understanding of technology, writing ability, and great people skills.

Docs for Developers: An Engineer's Field Guide to Technical Writing

This is my best and personal recommendation. Written by Jared Bhatti and co.

Learn to integrate programming with good documentation. This book teaches you the craft of documentation for each step in the software development lifecycle, from understanding your users' needs to publishing, measuring, and maintaining useful developer documentation.

Technical Writing: The Complete Guide

Docs for Developers demystifies the process of creating great developer documentation, following a team of software developers as they work to launch a new product. At each step along the way, you learn through examples, templates, and principles how to create, measure, and maintain documentation — tools you can adapt to the needs of your organization.

Managing Your Documentation Projects

This book helps you manage every phase of your publication and documentation projects. Written by JoAnn T. Hackos.

Practical, authoritative, and the first comprehensive guide to managing every phase of your publication project.

Technical Writing For Dummies

This is the most friendly guide to technical writing and I will personally recommend it to beginners and newbies to the Technical writing industry. Written by Sheryl Lindsell-Roberts.

Technical Writing Forums and Communities

The importance of communities in learning and growing as a technical writer cannot be overemphasized.

It helps you gain momentum, and gain connections and peers. It challenges you to do better every day. It gives you a sense of belonging and below is a list of technical writing communities you can join today.

Content/ry Community

The Contentry community is dedicated to helping you grow in your technical writing career. We provide tools, articles, videos, tips, webinars, and many resources to help you grow your technical writing career.

Hashnode Community

The Hashnode community hosts thousands of technical writers, who communicate, share, and network. It is a great place to connect with technical writers and like-minds.

The Writing Cooperative

The Writing Cooperative is a great resource for writers and the writing community on Medium. You should follow them to learn more about writing.

WriteTheDocs

Write the Docs is a large community of writers and documentation writers. It is a place for writers to share ideas, learn and grow together. You can join the Slack channel now.

Technical Writing Jobs

Getting your first job as a technical writer requires a lot of work, from creating and selecting intriguing samples, to creating an eye-catching software marketing portfolio.

Below is a list of tips to help you accelerate your technical writing job:

1. Create and Publish up to 3 - 5 technical content samples.
2. Create a personalized technical portfolio using [software].
3. **Create a detailed Content Brief:** The content brief should detail everything your content will cover, the target audience, the goal of the content, the primary and secondary keywords, and most importantly how that content will be useful to the audience of the company you're applying to.
4. **Create a good Content Proposal:** The proposal should contain link to your personalized portfolio containing only samples related to the topic you proposed. It should also contain the content brief.
5. Email or apply to the company with the proposal.

Additionally, you can use a complete guide on how to create a Great Technical Writing Article from scratch.

Here is also a list of companies currently hiring and in need of remote technical writers.

Technical Writing: The Complete Guide

Introducing Contentre

Contentre helps technical writers grow and gain more clients. Grow your technical writing career in one place.

Now that you're here, let me briefly recap the most important features Contentre can offer you:

- Organize your content in categories, topics, and tags Create and manage multiple clients.
- Create and manage multiple personalized portfolios
- Get statistical analytics of your content revenue, top categories, and tags.
- Easily generate content outlines, content briefs for your new project.
- Easily create content proposals or cover letter that stands out to your clients.
- And lot more

I highly recommend you try out Contentre. It will save you a tons of time with repeated tasks such as creating and managing different personalized portfolios, creating content outlines, creating content briefs, creating content proposals/cover letters, organizing all your technical content in one place.

Try it now. It's free

Final Words

Technical writing is a booming field and continues to be a highly coveted skill in the professional workplace.

The demand for technical writers is expected to grow by 10% from 2014 to 2024 faster than the average for all occupations.

This guide has detailed everything you need to become a technical writer, from knowing what technical writing is all about to understand the job of a technical writer.

If you enjoy this book consider rating the book 5-star and sharing the download link with your friends and social media.

Do you have questions, reviews or suggestions. Send it to adiaronojoete@gmail.com

Made in the USA
Middletown, DE
13 April 2023